# ENDING HARASSMENT AND RETALIATION IN THE WORKPLACE USING SCIENCE

By Jennifer Hancock

Published by Jennifer Hancock

Copyright 2018 by Jennifer Hancock
Published 2018
CreateSpace Edition
ISBN-13: 978-1987765762
ISBN-10: 1987765761

This book is also available in print at most online retailers

All rights reserved. No part of this book may be used or reproduced in any manner whatsoever without written permission, except in the case of brief quotations embodied in critical articles or reviews.

This ebook is licensed for your personal enjoyment only. This ebook may not be re-sold or given away to other people. If you would like to share this book with another person, please purchase an additional copy for each recipient.

~~~~~

# Table of Contents

CHAPTER 1: INTRODUCTION: WHY THIS BOOK? ......... 5

CHAPTER 2: WHAT IS HARASSMENT? ......................... 7

CHAPTER 3: WHY DOES RETALIATION HAPPEN? ......... 9

CHAPTER 4: THE SCIENCE BEHIND HOW TO MAKE IT STOP ...................................................................... 13

CHAPTER 5: REINFORCING TO OUR ADVANTAGE ...... 17

CHAPTER 6: AN OVERVIEW OF THE BEHAVIORAL EXTINCTION PROCESS ................................................ 21

CHAPTER 7: HOW TO GET HARASSMENT TO STOP ... 23

CHAPTER 8: ENDING HARASSMENT & RETALIATION IN THE WORKPLACE USING SCIENCE .............................. 29

CHAPTER 9: ABOUT THE AUTHOR: ........................... 31

# CHAPTER 1: INTRODUCTION: WHY THIS BOOK?

This is the companion book to the online courses *Ending Harassment & Retaliation in the Workplace.*

This program teaches how to use operant conditioning (behavioral conditioning techniques) to extinguish unwanted behaviors such as bullying or harassment in the workplace. This book provides an overview of the technique and how to use it to extinguish unwanted behaviors.

This is the transcript for the *Ending Harassment & Retaliation in the Workplace* course which is a one-hour program that is good for individuals who are being harassed or anyone who is interested in learning the basics of how to control the retaliation dynamic. Groups can also benefit from this course, which can be used as the basis of a sexual harassment training. For more information on this course visit:
https://humanistlearning.com/retaliation1/

This book contains transcripts of the course for easy home reference.

# Ending Harassment & Retaliation in the Workplace

Harassment occurs in many forms; and almost always, attempts to get it to stop results in some form of retaliation.

This book will discuss what harassment is, and why retaliation happens so that we can better understand the retaliation dynamic as a process. Understanding why and how retaliation occurs will help us understand what has to happen to get it to stop.

~~~~~

# CHAPTER 2: WHAT IS HARASSMENT?

There are several definitions of harassment. I'm going to start with the one I prefer most. Florida state law defines harassment as "a course of conduct directed at a specific person which causes substantial emotional distress to that person and serves no legitimate purpose."

It goes on to say, "Course of conduct means a pattern of conduct composed of a series of acts over a period of time, however short, which evidences a continuity of purpose. The term does not include constitutionally protected activity such as picketing or other organized protests."

A single obnoxious statement, no matter how rude it is, is not harassment. A series of obnoxious statements designed to denigrate a person over a period of time is harassment.

You might wonder why I started with state law. The reason is because in Florida (as in most states) harassment, when it is done willfully, maliciously and repeatedly is considered a crime. That crime is *stalking*, which is why most states have legal definitions of what harassment is.

You may have noticed that this definition does not concern itself with the reasons why it is happening or with what form the harassment takes. If you intentionally inflict emotional harm on someone for no good purpose, you have harassed them.

# Harassment in the Workplace

In the workplace certain forms of harassment are illegal whether they rise to the level of stalking or not. Specifically, it is illegal to harass someone because of race, color, religion, sex (gender), national origin, age (over 40), and/or disability. These forms of harassment are illegal when they create a hostile work environment or when enduring such harassment become a condition of continued employment.

What is interesting about these protected classes is that they pretty much match the targets of verbal bullying exactly. Dr. Lieberman at MIT did a study on verbal and cyber bullying and he found that 95% of all verbal bullying was about 6 things.

These 6 things are: race, ethnicity, sex, appearance, intelligence, and social inclusion or exclusion. (see: http://www.theatlantic.com/magazine/archive/2013/03/how-to-stop-bullies/309217/)

There is a reason these 6 things are used as insults and to denigrate others so often. Harassment is really just an adult form of bullying.

~~~~~

# CHAPTER 3: WHY DOES RETALIATION HAPPEN?

As pretty much everyone knows, if you stand up to a bully or a harasser, you are almost assuredly going to experience retaliation. This is why as much as we are told to report things, most of us don't.

We know that if we report what is happening our situation isn't likely to improve ... and ... reporting will probably make things worse.

The good news is that not only is retaliation predictable, we know why it happens and what it takes to get it to stop. The bad news is that it isn't easy to stop.

## The Behavioral Extinction Process

It turns out that retaliation is actually part of the behavioral extinction process. We have learned from decades of behavioral studies that unlearning a behavior follows a very predictable pattern. This pattern is called the extinction process.

(Note: because there is literally decades of research on this phenomenon all of which verify this is what happens, I am not going to cite a specific study but rather refer you to the Wikipedia article here: https://en.wikipedia.org/wiki/Extinction_(psychology) ) as well as linking to the 33,400+ scholarly articles on behavioral extinction using operant conditioning - https://scholar.google.com/scholar?q=operant+conditioning+extinction&btnG=&hl=en&as_sdt=0%2C10&as_vis=1 and the 26,000+ articles on BF Skinner and operant conditioning techniques - https://scholar.google.com/scholar?q=Skinner+operant+conditioning&btnG=&hl=en&as_sdt=0%2C10&as_vis=1)

What has been learned from all this research is that the behavioral extinction process is the same whether you are extinguishing smoking behavior or getting a dog to stop barking. You eliminate the reward received for the behavior. This triggers an extinction burst which is an escalation of behavior (which people being harassed experience as retaliation). You continue to not reward the unwanted behavior despite the increased attempts by the animal or organism to get their reward back (this is the hard part) and eventually the animal blows out and the behavior is extinguished.

All unlearning follows this pattern. Every species studied follows this pattern, including humans. And in case you were wondering, you do this too.

# You do this too/Breaking the habit

To better understand what is happening and why this escalation/retaliation is beyond the control of the person you have asked to stop. Let's consider how hard it is to break a habit.

Let's imagine that you work in an office and every day at 2 pm you go to a vending machine and get yourself a candy bar. Then, one day you go to the vending machine, put in your money, punch the buttons and nothing happens. Nothing moves. No coils turn. The machine is broken. What do you do?

Most people will press some more buttons. Some may try to shove the machine. Some may even get violent with it. How violent you get depends entirely on how aggressive your basic personality is, how long you have been getting candy bars from this machine and how addicted you are to your afternoon sugar. But no one walks away without at least attempting to get the machine to work.

Bullying is the same. The bully presses their victim's buttons. The victim responds. If the victim stops responding, the bully gets more aggressive to get the victim to respond again.

Retaliation occurs because harassment is a form of bullying and bullying is all about control. People do not give up control very easily and they certainly don't give it up without a fight. Just like people don't give up their vending machine treat without a fight.

If you are going to eliminate harassment you have to control the retaliation dynamic which is actually the extinction process and there is only one protocol that works to do this. Deviate from this protocol and you will not only fail to eliminate the harassment, you will make thing worse. This can be done, but it isn't easy to do.

~~~~~

# CHAPTER 4: THE SCIENCE BEHIND HOW TO MAKE IT STOP

## Reinforcements: Rewards and Punishments

In order to eliminate harassment and control the retaliation dynamic that is triggered when we remove the reward, we have to understand the extinction protocol better. We need to have a better understanding of what constitutes rewards and punishments and we have to learn about reinforcement schedules. Don't worry this is easier than it sounds.

There are three types of reinforcements:

- Positive – where the animal likes what just happened.
- Negative – where they don't.
- And neutral – which is neither positive nor negative.

(Note: if you have a background in behavioral psychology please be aware I am using these terms differently than their technical meanings. In this case negative is being used to describe punishment and I am substituting neutral for negative. This is done intentionally to make the concepts easily understandable to a lay audience.)

When you train an animal – you use a combination of positive, negative and neutral responses to get the animal to do what you want them to do. This is called operant conditioning.

Most people have an instinctual understanding of the power of positive and negative reinforcements. However, they usually completely forget that they also have the option to not reinforce at all which is what the neutral response provides.

The neutral response is critical to the behavioral extinction process. If you want to extinguish an unwanted behavior, you have to provide a neutral response. This is counter intuitive so I will repeat it. The most effective way to eliminate unwanted behavior is the neutral response. If you negatively reinforce or punish a harasser you actually strengthen the unwanted behavior because negative reinforcement is still reinforcement. This is why no good trainer uses punishment and why hitting a child is now considered immoral.

The neutral response is so effective that almost all advice on how to stop a bully is "ignore them and they will go away." What this really means is respond to them in a neutral way and they will eventually go away after they escalate their behavior for a bit.

## Reinforcement Schedules

A reinforcement schedule is how often you give out rewards or punishments for behavior. There are two basic ways you can reinforce an animal: consistently or variably.

- Consistent reinforcement is when you reward or punish every single time.
- Variable is when you reinforce every once in a while.

When you reinforce and how often you reinforce has a HUGE impact on how strongly an animal associates the reward with the behavior. This is again counterintuitive, but responding in a variable way strengthens the behavior, whether you want it to or not. Consistent reinforcement leads to a weaker behavior. Every study ever done on behavioral dynamics has shown this to be true.

~~~~~

# CHAPTER 5: REINFORCING TO OUR ADVANTAGE

We can use this knowledge, about how and when to reinforce, to our advantage.

If we want to weaken our harassers desire to harass us, we need to consistently use a neutral reinforcement schedule. If all we ever do is respond 100% consistently, our situation will improve and the harasser will harass less.

To make this work we must give our bully the exact same response every single time. Not just every once in a while. Every single time! Unfortunately, we humans are rarely consistent.

I want you to understand how incredibly important it is to remain consistent when extinguishing a behavior. When you variably reinforce a bully, you strengthen their resolve to bully. It makes the bullying worse! And not just a little bit worse, a lot worse.

In fact, most of the escalation that occurs in harassment situations is because the victim tries to "ignore" the bully or harasser for a bit. The bully escalates and retaliates as predicted by the behavioral extinction model. The victim gives up because their attempt to ignore the bully didn't work so they start responding to the bully again. The cycle then repeats, every time getting a little bit worse. This is the definition of variable reinforcement! Variable reinforcement makes things worse.

Being consistent is critical to the entire extinction process. It isn't just that by being consistent we will weaken the unwanted behavior. There is another even more important reason why consistency matters.

And that is ... the extinction burst.

## Blowouts and Extinction Bursts

When we break any habit, we all go through an extinction burst. When an animal doesn't get their reward, they escalate their behavior. If they still don't get their reward they escalate some more. Eventually their behavior becomes incredibly obnoxious and almost constant as the animal makes a last ditch attempt to get their reward back. This extreme behavior is called the extinction burst or blow out. Animal trainers prefer the term blow out because it more accurately describes what it is like to experience it.

For example: imagine we have a rat that has been trained to push a button to get some food. One day the lever doesn't work. The rat will push the button more and more. This is the predicted escalation of behavior. Eventually, they will get to the point where they are pushing the button almost constantly. They are literally desperate to get their reward back. This frantic behavior is the extinction burst or blow out.

The bad news is that it is really obnoxious. The good news is that when you get to this point, you are almost done.

When we apply this to bullies, we see them doing some level of bullying, and when we stop allowing them to get away with it they escalate their behavior. If we aren't consistent and give in before the harasser completes the extinction process, we are left with a new norm which is an escalated level of aggressive behavior!

This dynamic is the main reason why it is so hard to get harassment and workplace bullying to stop. This is why most people are convinced that efforts to get harassment to stop not only don't work, they make things worse. They do make things worse, but only because they didn't complete the extinction process.

What is happening is that people do the right thing. They neutrally reinforce. This triggers the extinction process and the harasser escalates their behavior (and yes, retaliation is part of that escalation to regain control and rewards). But because the victim isn't aware that the escalation is evidence that what they are doing is actually working, they give up before the extinction process is complete and things continue on as they had before – only worse and at a more aggressive level.

Typically, what happens is that this cycle repeats through a series of uncompleted extinction bursts and an accidental variable reinforcement schedule, which we all tend to fall into.

~~~~~

## CHAPTER 6: AN OVERVIEW OF THE BEHAVIORAL EXTINCTION PROCESS

# Extinguishing a Behavior: The Protocol

In order to extinguish a behavior you have to:

- Provide a neutral response to the behavior you want to extinguish
- Be 100% consistent in your response
- Ride the blow out or extinction burst until the behavior is extinguished.

Simple right? Not really.

When an animal blows out they are escalating their behavior. The reason it's called a blowout is because right before they give up, they throw everything they've got to get their reward back. Part of the blow out behavior for humans is retaliation!

The good news is when you get to this point, you are nearly done. The bad news is, it's really hard to remain firm at this point. We are humans, not broken vending machines. The pressure gets to us. It is usually at this point that people give in.

To get it to stop. Don't give in.

~~~~~

# CHAPTER 7: HOW TO GET HARASSMENT TO STOP

A victim of harassment is limited in what they can do. They must have help. If they don't get that help, they will fail. Let's talk about what has to happen in the workplace to support the extinction process.

A victim's role is to respond in a neutral unemotional way to alert the harasser that what they did wasn't ok. It is best if they have a practiced prepared statement to say out loud: something along the lines of, "that isn't acceptable behavior."

It is critical that this statement be made calmly, rationally and without emotion. Most people have to practice this and role-play; so that in the moment, they will respond appropriately, and as they have planned.

The victim must also report what has happened every single time. Harassment and/or bullying in the workplace is a legal matter so properly documenting the harassment is key. Because harassment is a pattern of behavior, we need to document every incident to show evidence of that pattern. Documentation logs are very helpful in this regard. (Here is a link to a sample log you can use - http://thebullyvaccine.com/downloads/documentationlog.pdf)

It isn't enough to complain once and expect the problem to go away. All that will do is trigger an extinction burst and escalate the problem. This is a process that will take place over time and the harasser will most likely escalate their behavior and retaliate.

Knowing this in advance means you can be prepared for it to happen. As soon as you realize you have a problem, start documenting everything that goes on.

The other reason to fully document what is happening is because it is very easy for managers and EEO officers to brush off one-time complaints. It is much harder for them to look at a properly documented pattern of harassment and not do anything about it. If they don't take action, you will have the documentation you need to file a legal claim.

# Harassment Does Not Occur in a Vacuum

Harassment/bullying and retaliation do not occur in a vacuum. Other people are involved as well. Co-workers and bystanders who witness this behavior must be empowered to respond and intervene in real time to let the harasser know what they did was not ok.

We all have a tendency to let things slide, but this actually rewards the harasser and emboldens them because it not only creates a variable reinforcement pattern, it also creates a cultural norm of acceptance and silence. What we want to do is create a new cultural norm where that sort of behavior is not accepted.

It is critical that victims know that others support them. It's what gives them the courage to ride out the blow out. It is also important that the harasser knows that the status they were hoping to get by denigrating a co-worker is not only not materializing, their status has actually been harmed by their behavior.

To discourage harassers, bystanders must speak out – in a calm rational way – to let a bully know what they did was not ok. As with victims – it is important to have something you have planned to say and to have practiced it. It is simple enough to say – "that's not appropriate behavior in the workplace."

Tone of voice should be neutral, calm and compassionate with an expectation that the harasser will behave themselves.

And yes, you do have to risk retaliation and becoming a target yourself if you do this. Understand that the harasser/bully is trying to control everyone through aggression. The only way to stop it is to stop allowing them to do this which means you have to be willing to stand up and stop rewarding them with your silence and compliance.

Bystanders and co-workers have the most power to stop harassment in the workplace if they are committed to the process and consistent in creating a cultural norm where harassment simply isn't tolerated. It just takes one or two people to create a new cultural norm. Be that person. Take this on.

## Managers/HR and EEO Officers

Managers, HR staff and EEO officers also have an important role to play. They are responsible for making sure that there is not only an adequate reporting process, but that their response to these reports supports the extinction process instead of making things worse.

When things are first reported, our instinct is to treat this as a conflict and to be lenient as a result. We rarely treat these reports as what they really are, a pattern of harassment. What we don't realize is that this leniency sets up a variable reinforcement scenario that accelerates and compounds the problem and makes it worse.

Bullying and harassment isn't to be tolerated, ever. No exceptions. No, "We'll let it go this time." Every incident must be dealt with consistently and fairly, every time. The response must be immediate (or as immediate as your processes allow) and documentation for legal purposes must be thorough.

## If you are a Victim

- Respond Neutrally
- Report and document everything
- Understand that this is a process that will take place over time
- Be consistent and persistent for as long as it takes
- Expect retaliation
- Don't stop until it stops.

Once you trigger an extinction burst, you must see it through to the end. To stop in the middle because it gets too hard means the harasser has won and it creates a new more aggressive level of harassment against you. Do not start this process unless you are committed to seeing it through.

## If you are a manager

- Believe the victim
- Expect the accused to retaliate
- Monitor their behavior over time
- Be consistent with your consequences
- Document everything – this is critical to establish the pattern of behavior that is harassment
- Don't be lenient – leniency creates variable reinforcement which makes things worse.

It's actually more compassionate to be strict when it comes to inappropriate behavior. You will cycle through the extinction process quicker if you are strict and consistent.

~~~~~

# CHAPTER 8: ENDING HARASSMENT & RETALIATION IN THE WORKPLACE USING SCIENCE

The key to understanding why it is so hard to get bullies and harassers to stop is to understand how we unlearn behaviors. Workplace bullying and harassment doesn't arise out of thin air. These are behaviors that has been learned and rewarded for the entire life of the aggressor. It worked in grade school and all the way through high school.

For most serial harassers this sort of behavior is an adaptive strategy to get what they want. They think it works, that's why they do it! When you encounter a workplace bully, you pretty much have to assume, this isn't new behavior. This is part of a pattern of behavior and there isn't a single victim, but rather multiple victims.

By the time it's reported to a manager – it's already a serious problem! In order to get it to stop, several things have to happen.

These steps are what are known as extinguishing a behavior, and it is a standard operant conditioning technique.

- Stop rewarding the unwanted behavior.
- Increase the cost associated with performing the unwanted behavior
- Ride the blow out by being 100% consistent in not providing a reward despite repeatedly more aggressive attempts to get a reward
- Reward the behavior you do want (provide an alternative way to get a reward)
- Nip in the bud any future attempts to re-establish the unwanted behavior

~~~~~

# CHAPTER 9: ABOUT THE AUTHOR:

Jennifer Hancock is a mom, author of several books, and founder of Humanist Learning Systems. Jennifer is unique in that she was raised as a freethinker and is considered one of the top speakers and writers in the world of Humanism today. Her professional background is varied including stints in both the for profit and non-profit sectors. She has served as Director of Volunteer Services for the Los Angeles SPCA, sold international franchise licenses for a biotech firm, was the Manager of Acquisition Group Information for a ½ billion-dollar company and served as the executive director for the Humanists of Florida. When she became a mother, she decided to stay at home, but that didn't last long. Shortly after her son was born, she published her first book, *The Humanist Approach to Happiness: Practical Wisdom*. Her speaking and teaching business coalesced into the founding of Humanist Learning Systems which provides online personal and professional development training in humanistic business management and science based harassment training that actually works.

## *More Learning from Jennifer Hancock*

## Other books by Jennifer Hancock

- The Humanist Approach to Happiness
- Jen Hancock's Handy Humanism Handbook
- The Bully Vaccine
- The Humanist Approach to Grief and Grieving
- How to Win Arguments Without Arguing
- Why Bullies Bully & How to Stop Them Using Science
- Reality Based Decision Making for Effective Strategy Development

## Courses taught by Jennifer Hancock

- Workplace Bullying for HR professionals
- Living Made Simpler
- An Introduction to Humanism
- Socratic Jujitsu: How to Win Arguments Without Argument
- Why Conflict Resolution Doesn't Work When the Problem is Bullying
- Bridging the Generational Divide: Millennials vs. Boomers
- Ending Harassment and Retaliation in the Workplace

- [Reality Based Decision Making for Effective Strategy Development](#)
- [How to De-escalate Conflicts Using Behavioral Science](#)
- [Why is Change so Hard?](#)
- [Principles of Humanistic Management](#)
- [7 Sins of Staff Management](#)
- [How to Handle Cranky Customer Problems](#)
- [New Manager Orientation](#)
- [Humanist Group Leadership Lessons](#)
- [Sexual harassment training that works – general](#)
- [Sexual harassment training that works – AB 1825](#)
- [Stop Bullying in our Workplace – Staff Training](#)
- [Sexual Harassment Compliance Training](#)
- [No Fear Act training](#)
- [Planning for Personal Success!](#)
- [Talking to your child about death](#)
- [The Bully Vaccine Toolkit](#)
- [How to talk to your child's school about bullying](#)
- [Why Bullies Bully & How to Stop Them](#)

***Connect with Me Online:***

- Twitter: http://twitter.com/#!/JentheHumanist
- Facebook: http://www.facebook.com/JentheHumanist
- Or sign up for my mailing list: http://eepurl.com/c3LuI

#####

www.ingramcontent.com/pod-product-compliance
Lightning Source LLC
Chambersburg PA
CBHW030103230526
45471CB00003B/1236